ILLUSTRATED BY

COVER -UP

A Curious History of Clothes Uncovered

by Richard Tames esq.

MARK DRAISEY

MACDONALD YOUNG BOOKS

CONTENTS

First published in 1995 by Macdonald Young Books Ltd
© Text Richard Tames 1995
© Illustration Macdonald Young Books Ltd 1995

Macdonald Young Books Ltd
Campus 400
Maylands Avenue
Hemel Hempstead
Herts HP2 7EZ

Commissioning editor   Debbie Fox
Design   Roger Kohn
Editor   Diana Russell
DTP editor   Helen Swansbourne
Illustrator   Mark Draisey
Illustrator's agent   Funny Business

A CIP catalogue record for this book is available from
the British Library

ISBN: 0 7500 1567 5

"Printed in Portugal by Edições ASA"

THE HISTORY OF CLOTHES

Warfare
● In the 4th century BC, Alexander the Great *BANNED* his soldiers from wearing beards, because they would give enemies something to grab in close combat!

Materials
● The punch-hole pattern on *brogue shoes* is just for decoration nowadays. Originally the holes went right through the leather so that people walking through *IRISH BOGS* could let the water out easily when they got to dry ground.

Geography
● The 'dinner jacket' (called a *'tuxedo'* in America) was invented at Lake Tuxedo, New York. Denim is named after Nimes in France and jeans after Genoa in Italy.

Religion
● In the Middle Ages, priests disapproved of people wearing *WIGS*. The priests said that if they put their hands on someone's head to give a blessing, the blessing wouldn't go through if the person was wearing a wig!

Languages
● The word *'umbrella'* comes from the Latin for 'shade'. *'Parasol'* literally means 'against sun'.

Public finance
● As part of his drive to modernize Russia, Peter the Great (1682–1721) ordered his nobles to *SHAVE OFF* their beards. Peasants and priests could keep them if they paid a *BEARD TAX*.

Hygiene
● The 16th-century French General de Coligny used to store *SPARE TOOTHPICKS* in his beard!
● Josephine, wife of French Emperor Napoleon (1804–1815), changed her underwear *THREE TIMES* a day!

Natural history
● The arrival of the first giraffes at London Zoo in the 1830s sparked off a craze for dappled cloth!

Child care
● The ancient Cretans made their children wear *TIGHT GIRDLES* to give them narrow waists.
● The Native American Chinook tribe used to bind their babies' heads to *WOODEN PLANKS* to elongate their skulls.
● When America's first President, George Washington (1789–97), ordered a new set of clothes for his four-year-old step-daughter, the shopping list ran to *59* items!

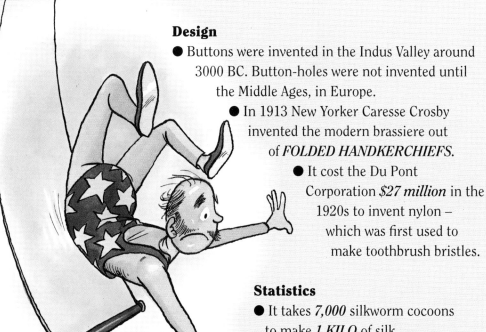

Inventors

● Leotards are named after the French trapeze artist who invented them. Other inventors' names include Macintosh, Burberry, Cardigan and Stetson.

Chemistry

● Elizabeth 1's (1558–1603) favourite hair gel was made from apples and *PUPPY FAT*. To imitate her auburn hair, her courtiers shampooed theirs with white wine and rhubarb.

● Native Americans learned that one of the best materials for making buckskin super-soft was *ANIMAL BRAINS*.

● Dry-cleaning was invented in 1849 when a Frenchman knocked a spirit lamp over a table-cloth and saw the *STAINS* on it disappear.

Nutrition

● Victorian women cultivated a pale complexion by drinking *VINEGAR!*

Sport

● Baseball caps were once worn pointing *FORWARDS!*

Design

● Buttons were invented in the Indus Valley around 3000 BC. Button-holes were not invented until the Middle Ages, in Europe.

● In 1913 New Yorker Caresse Crosby invented the modern brassiere out of *FOLDED HANDKERCHIEFS.*

● It cost the Du Pont Corporation *$27 million* in the 1920s to invent nylon – which was first used to make toothbrush bristles.

Statistics

● It takes *7,000* silkworm cocoons to make *1 KILO* of silk.

● Over three years, the average French woman buys four brassieres, an English woman buys nine and an American 15.

People

● South American Incas wore earlobe plugs made of wool, reeds, straw or gold. Some were up to *15 cm* across. Officials whose ears burst under the strain were demoted.

● When Louis XIV's army occupied Strasbourg in 1681, local people were given four months to switch over to dressing like the French!

Look how much you've learned already!

And that was only

THE INTRODUCTION!

Ancient Egyptians had two basic styles of dressing – **with** clothes and **without**. The climate was either warm, hot or very hot. So children, servants and labourers went naked! Even the wealthy just wore loin cloths, kilts or shift-dresses. As Egypt is 90% sand, dressing for the beach made sense – and cut down on laundry!

HAVE YOU SEEN MY MUMMY?

Dying to look your best

When wealthy people died, they were prepared for the after-life by a process of embalming which took 70 days. The heart, liver and other internal organs were taken out and preserved separately in a special set of jars. The brain wasn't kept; it was *SCRAPED OUT* bit by bit, using hooks forced up the nose! The body was then stuffed with mineral crystals, which dried out all its fluids. This meant no moisture was left to feed bacteria – so the body wouldn't rot! The face was often made up and padded out to look healthy, with false eyes made of *ROCK-CRYSTAL* to replace the real ones. Finger-nails were *SEWN ON* to stop them falling off. Finally, the body was wrapped in up to 5 kilometres of linen bandages and placed inside two or three coffins. The word 'mummy' comes from the Arabic name for the resin ('mum') used to stick the bandages together.

Would you like it in white – *OR WHITE?*

Unless vegetable dyes are 'fixed' with a special chemical, they soon wash out. The Egyptians didn't catch on to this and so had to leave their linen garments their natural colour – *OFF-WHITE*. To liven things up, they added lots of flowers, jewels and ribbons.

Which one shall I wear today?

Pharaohs wore *FALSE BEARDS*, tied on with string, to make them look old, wise, fierce and important. Some were made of hair with gold thread woven in for a sparkly effect. Some were made of metal shavings! *QUEENS* wore beards too when they were officially on duty!

Look cool! Feel cool!

Men and women both wore wigs to protect their heads from the fierce sun. The best ones were made from *REAL HAIR* and the cheapest from flax or even palm leaves! Beeswax was used to set wigs in braids or curls. Outdoors, people covered their wigs with a cloth to stop the wax melting and to keep the dust off. At dinner-parties, really smart women wore a cone of perfumed wax on their heads, so that it gradually melted and released the perfume!

Sole survivors

Most Egyptians went barefoot around the house. For outdoors, they had sandals made of leather or woven rushes. On journeys they often carried their sandals, so they wouldn't be spoilt.

The Hollywood version

Cleopatra, made in 1963, was the longest (over four hours) and most expensive (*$40 MILLION*) Hollywood epic ever made. Elizabeth Taylor, who played Cleopatra, wore a black wig (*CORRECT!*), but it had straight hair (*WRONG!*) when it should have been curly. And to be *really* authentic Liz should have worn her wig on top of a shaved head – which should have been oiled to make it shiny!

After you with the eye-liner!

★ Men *AND* women wore cosmetics.
★ As pale colours reflect light, grey or green eye-liner was used to ward off the glare of the sun.
★ On festive occasions, henna was used to stain red decorative patterns on the palms of the hands and soles of the feet.
★ Castor-oil was used as a sun-tan lotion, and there were preparations to treat dandruff, baldness, spots and wrinkles.
★ One recipe for hair dye recommends mixing the *BLOOD OF A BLACK COW* with a blend of *CRUSHED TADPOLES.*

Footing the bill

In 1977 General Bokassa, ruler of the Central African Republic, crowned himself emperor. His coronation shoes, studded with pearls, cost *$85,000!*

Best foot *fore! ward*

The most expensive footwear regularly on sale is made by Stylo Matchmakers of Northampton. Their *MINK-LINED* golf shoes have *REAL GOLD* trimmings and spikes tipped with *RUBIES.* In 1992 they cost *£13,200* a pair. Of course, there's no guarantee you'll play any better in them!

Snow go!

Snow-shoe racing is popular in Canada. A top racer can cover 100 yards (91.4 metres) in *12 SECONDS!*

BEST FOOT FORWARD

They give you a *LIFT!*

High heels appeared around 1580. Many women also used *'pattens'*, wooden slippers 7–10 centimetres high, to keep their shoes clear of muddy roads. In 17th-century Venice they wore *'chopines'* – pattens up to *80 cm high!* Servants had to help women wearing them to keep their balance!

By the left ... or right?

From 1600 to about 1800 boots were made as *'straights'*, to be worn on either foot. Soldiers changed their boots over every day, to ensure they lasted as long as possible and wore out evenly!

Vintage stuff!

The 18th-century dandy Beau Brummell always had immaculate shining boots, but would never tell how his valet got such a gloss on them. Finally, he revealed the secret formula for his boot polish was *CHAMPAGNE!* And in the *very best* Victorian houses servants not only polished their master's shoes, they washed and ironed the *LACES* as well!

Wave goodbye!

In Japan, it's polite to take off your shoes before entering a house. When the first railway was demonstrated there in the 1870s, passengers *lined up* their shoes on the *platform* before boarding. Only as the train pulled away did they realise their shoes wouldn't be there to greet them at the journey's end!

Golden Boy

In 2nd-century Rome, Lucius Verus used to sprinkle *GOLD DUST* in his blond hair to make it look more dazzling!

Royal cover-up

Balding Louis XIII (1610–43) of France introduced the fashion for wigs. His son Louis XIV (1643–1715) thought wigs were ridiculous – until he went bald at 32 and changed his mind! Louis XIV's wigs were always *very* black until he got quite old, and let his barber sprinkle in a *little* powder to suggest he was a *tiny* bit grey!

IS **THAT** *REALLY* YOURS?

All change

Roman hair-styles were always changing, so rich ladies had their statues made with *SEPARATE HAIR-PIECES* which could be changed to match the latest fashion! They also wore blonde wigs made from the hair of German or British slaves.

I know you're in there somewhere

Ladies' hair-styles of the 1770s were so elaborately decorated with jewels, ribbons and bird-feathers, they were kept on for *THREE WEEKS* at a time. The sticks now sold as 'back-scratchers' were first made to get at *VERMIN* on the scalp! *MICE* climbed in when the wearer was asleep, and in 1777 a new silver bedside mousetrap won a prize for design!

Matt or gloss?

Roman men combed their hair forwards or wore wigs to hide baldness. Some bald men had their scalps *PAINTED BLACK* to look like hair!

Or use it for baking ...

During the 18th-century Revolutionary War, American soldiers were allowed *HALF A KILO* of flour a week to powder their wigs! Powdering was such a messy business that people used a special *powder room* for the purpose!

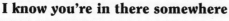

Ready to wear

When the English diary-writer Samuel Pepys bought a new wig, he found it was infected with *HEAD-LICE!* After the Great Plague of 1665, he recorded that cheap wigs were made from the hair of people who had *DIED IN THE EPIDEMIC!*

*The Greeks were clever people who were content with simple clothes and kept busy by quarrelling with their neighbours. The Romans were never content with anything and kept busy by **conquering** all their neighbours! Greek dress changed little over the centuries. The Romans changed THREE TIMES A DAY if they could! The Greek idea of 'simple' was a wool tunic with no embroidery. The Roman idea of 'simple' was **only** using gold to embroider a robe of purple silk!*

TUNICS & TOGAS

Here, rub this on

The Greek doctor Galen invented a facial treatment made of water, beeswax and olive oil. The water evaporated on contact with warm skin, giving a cooling effect – *THE WORLD'S FIRST COLD CREAM!* The Greeks also invented the first safety-pins; these were used to fasten cloaks.

Greeks and Romans had a horror of garments that had been sewn together, especially trousers, which were worn by their enemies, the Persians and the German tribes. As far as Greeks and Romans were concerned, trousers were for *SAVAGES* – the Romans even passed a law against them which carried *THE DEATH PENALTY!* Wool and linen were the most common cloths, but the Romans also imported cotton from India. Silk from China cost three times its weight in gold!

Beard not weird?

Most Greek men were clean-shaven, except for professors who grew beards to show they didn't care about fashion. As shaving-soap and steel razors didn't exist, shaving was a painful business – so perhaps the professors really *were* wise!

Keep it toga-ther

The Roman toga was over *6 METRES* long. It looked very dignified, but was awkward to wear and even *more* awkward to put on properly. It had no fastenings or pins, but was held in place by the way it was draped and folded. The richest households had a special slave whose main job was to help the men of the family arrange their togas. Some men had them very carefully draped to show off

Uniform issue

Roman soldiers wore drawers under their armour and tunics, especially when they were stationed in a cold, damp province like Britain, where the weather was much worse than in Rome. Even then Britain specialised in making long, thick cloaks with hoods, which were *excellent* for keeping off the constant rain.

Senators prefer blondes

Roman ladies greatly admired the blonde hair of their barbarian slaves, and often tried to bleach their own with a mixture of beechwood ash and goat's fat. Unfortunately, this often made their hair get thinner or even fall out altogether! To restore it, they used conditioning creams made from ingredients like bear's grease, deer marrow, pepper and *RATS' HEADS*.

Chalk was used as a basic make-up, with wine-dregs for rouge and burnt cork for eyebrow liner. Ladies with naturally dark skins tried to achieve a pale complexion by using a cream made of narcissus bulbs, honey, wheat, barley, lentils and eggs.

The poet Ovid warned Roman men not to sneak into their girlfriends' rooms at night, or they would find that the women's make-up had melted and was running down their faces in great streaks!

Ouch!

Roman men shaved without oil or soap and with a razor made of *IRON*, which did not give a good edge. To heal cuts, they used plasters made from lots of *SPIDERS' WEBS* soaked in oil and vinegar. Some men tried to avoid shaving by using creams to remove bristles, made from pitch, white wine ass's fat, *BAT'S BLOOD* or *POWDERED VIPER!*

scars they had got in battle. Togas were also very good at covering up a *BIG BELLY* or *SPINDLY LEGS!*

Togas were colour-coded to show whether the wearer was a free man, an aristocrat or a senator. Only the emperor's family was allowed to wear purple garments. Apart from anything else the dye, which was made from crushed insects, was *very* expensive.

It's written all over your face!

In traditional Chinese opera, *FACIAL HAIR* is the clue to the characters of the male parts:
★ Long white beard = wise old man
★ Full beard, made-up eyes = warrior or god
★ Thin, pencil line, pointed moustache = playboy, liar, fool.

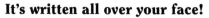

I've brought you this

After their first shave, Roman youths presented the gods with the cuttings in a bottle as a *THANK-OFFERING* for reaching manhood.

Rest easy

In 17th-century France, fashion-conscious men protected their carefully curled beards from creasing by wearing a *BOX* over them in bed!

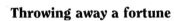

Beat that!

Birger Pellas of Sweden has the world's longest moustache – *2.86 METRES!*

Throwing away a fortune

K C Gillette invented the disposable *RAZOR BLADE* in 1903. He retired a millionaire in 1909!

Keep smiling!

In the 19th century, people thought luxurious whiskers were a sign of manliness. Young men were advised to rub their skin with *RAW ONION* to encourage the growth!

What do you call *THAT?*

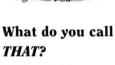

Bushy whiskers stretching from *EAR* to *JAW* are called '*sideburns*' after 19th-century American Civil War General Ambrose Burnside, who made them popular. Such whiskers were called '*cutlets*' in France and '*Piccadilly weepers*' in England.
Beard names included the *Barbed Wire*, *Billygoat* and *Hearthrug*. In the USA, thick moustaches were known as '*soup-strainers*'. Men in Britain used *SPECIALLY DESIGNED TEA-CUPS* to hoist their moustaches clear of their lips when they were drinking!

There's a mouse in the house!

In the 18th century, fashionable ladies with thin eyebrows could buy false eyebrows made of *MOUSE FUR!*

Modern sports gear began in the mid-19th century. Before then men played in their everyday clothes – and women just **didn't** play! As linen and undyed cotton were the cheapest materials for shirts, breeches, stockings and so on, this may explain why so many sports are played wearing *WHITE* – which is *GOOD NEWS* for makers of detergents and washing-machines! When fast-moving, body-contact sports, like various kinds of football, began to be played between teams on a regular basis, *BOLD PATTERNS* or *STRIPES* on shirts became essential so that you could know who your opponents were – and whose head you should try to rip off! Rules began to limit what you could do to WIN, WHERE you did it – and what you could WEAR.

IT'S ONLY A GAME!

Hat tricks

Until about 1850 cricketers wore *top hats*. (It was against the rules to use them to catch the ball!) If a bowler got three batsmen out with three successive balls, his team bought him a *NEW HAT* to celebrate! Today cricketers wear protective helmets instead.

Racing against time

Modern driving-suits give up to *50 SECONDS'* protection against the incredible heat of a petrol fire. They have reinforced *epaulets* to help rescuers pull a crashed driver clear of the wreckage. And helmets have a reserve supply of *COMPRESSED* air to save drivers from inhaling toxic fumes.

Navy blue

The '*blazer*' worn by many sports officials has nothing to do with sport as such! It was originally designed by the captain of the British ship HMS *Blazer* as a smart jacket for his crew – back in the 1840s before the Royal Navy had any set uniform for ordinary seamen!

Ice hockey

Ice hockey probably takes the record for protective gear. A goal-keeper can wear up to *19* different items!

Head cases

American football was first played by two colleges in 1869 – although there were no standard rules until 1873! In the early games there were *25* players on each side, but by 1880 this was reduced to 11. Injuries and deaths were so *common* that in 1905 President Theodore Roosevelt called for rule changes to make the game safer! Around 1910, players began to wear protective headgear based on leather flying helmets. Plastic helmets arrived in 1939. Modern helmets have *INFLATABLE SECTIONS* inside for added protection!

Phew! Unlike the Romans, who tried to bathe every day, the people of medieval Europe often went YEARS without having a bath. As they didn't have Roman-style central heating either, they usually wore heavy clothes, even indoors. So they were probably pretty smelly! Things began to get a bit fresher after the Crusades. Crusaders returning from the Middle East brought back the fashion for baths, perfumes, cosmetics and lightweight cloth.

The Muddle Ages

Just let me slip this on
Viking armoured shirts weighed about *15 – 20 KILOS*. The best way to put one on was to crawl into it and get a friend to pull you upright!

He's gone berserk!
The word *'berserk'* comes from the Vikings, who went into battle wearing a shirt (serk) of armour. But these shirts were very heavy and made it difficult to swing an axe with your full strength. So some Viking warriors wore bearskins instead – hence *be(a)rserk*!

Miaow-vellous!
Between 1095 and 1300, knights from western Europe fought to get control of Jerusalem and the Holy Land. The wars were called Crusades because the knights used a Christian cross ('crux' in Latin) as their badge. In the end the local Muslim rulers threw them out, but contact with the Middle East had a great influence on European fashion. Its warm climate meant light, flowing garments were more comfortable than thick, heavy ones. Returning Crusaders brought back bales of lightweight cloth as presents. The cloth was often named for the city where it was made. 'MUSLIN' was from Mosul in Iraq, 'DAMASK' from Damascus in Syria. 'TABBY', now only used to describe a kind of cat, was originally a kind of mottled pattern woven in Attabiyah in Iraq! Veils and buttons were also brought to Europe by Crusaders who had seen them in the Middle East.

I believe you dropped this

The Order of Knights of the Garter was founded by Edward III (1327–77), after the lady he was dancing with lost her stocking-garter! When his courtiers sniggered at this, the king said that one day any knight would be proud to wear a garter, because he would give it as a badge to the bravest of them.

Joust a minute!

Knights fought mock-battles called jousts to keep in practice – and to show off. Some gambled their armour on the outcome, and lost it if they lost the joust! In time, special jousting-armour, much heavier than battle-armour (and *that* weighed *25 KILOS!*), was designed to keep injuries to a minimum. Horse and rider wore the same patterned cloth, so spectators could identify them.

What's the point?

It is said that pointed shoes were introduced in Britain at the time of William II (1087–1100) by a man with deformed feet! By the 14th century this fashion had become very popular in the Polish city of Krakow, so pointed shoes were known as 'krakowes'. Priests were against them; they said they made it difficult for people to kneel down properly and say their prayers! Edward III passed laws saying that points should be no longer than 2 inches (5 centimetres). Nobody took any notice. So he passed another law saying not longer than 9 inches (23 cm). Nobody took much notice of that either! At its most extreme, the fashion led to shoes with points *TWICE* that long, stiffened with whalebone and attached to the knees with chains. Some had bells on! Even knights had their armour made with long points on the foot-coverings.

What did you say it was made of?

Armour has been made of:

★ leather boiled in wax

★ wickerwork

★ the skins of jaguars, crocodiles, armadillos and rhinoceroses

★ quilted cotton and silk

★ whalebone, ivory, horn and bark.

DRESSED TO KILL

Smooth as silk

12th-century Mongol warriors wore thick *SILK* shirts into battle. When they were hit by arrows, these drove the silk into the flesh rather than *penetrating* it! This made it easier to get the arrow-heads out afterwards!

What have you got on underneath?

Thick padded garments had to be worn under *CHAIN MAIL*; or a blow from a *SWORD* or *AXE* would drive the mail into your flesh! Rust spots were cleaned off chain mail by rolling it in a barrel of *FINE SAND!*

No, I'm sure this bit goes here ...

By the 16th century armour came in *garnitures* (kit-form sets), allowing the wearer to use different items according to whether he was fighting on foot or horseback and which weapons he carried. Archduke Maximilian II of Austria had a garniture of *123* items which could make up *12* different suits of armour!

Tie-up

'Cravat' comes from the French word for the neck-scarves worn by Croatians in the 17-century French army. The modern tie is a slimmed-down version!

Keep it under your hat!

Long after soldiers gave up wearing armour, they wore *IRON SKULL-CAPS* under their felt hats. These were known as *'secrets'* – hence the warning when someone told you a secret that you should keep it under your hat!

Helmet-a-soup

When he was camping out with his armies, the great 17th-century French General Turenne used to eat his soup out of his *HELMET!* This is why large silver soup-dishes are known as *'tureens'*!

Bard-of-Avon calling!

In 1886 an American salesman called David McConnell was trying to make a living by selling volumes of Shakespeare from door to door. To promote sales, he began giving away small bottles of *PERFUME* with each book sold. He soon found that more housewives were interested in *perfumes* than *plays* – and quickly went into making cosmetics! He then hit on the brilliant idea of using housewives as his *SALES FORCE* – to work part-time selling door-to-door to other housewives. Fifty-three years and a fortune later, McConnell changed the name of his Californian Perfume Company in honour of Shakespeare's birthplace and called it – AVON!

It's a cover-up!

Hogwash!

Queen Elizabeth I had the reputation of being very fussy about hygiene because, according to one surprised chronicler, she took a bath *TWICE A YEAR* – 'whether she needed to or not!'

It was quite different for Jane Lewson. Her husband died when she was 26 and after that she *never* washed again, because she thought it would make her catch a cold or something worse! Instead she settled for greasing her face and neck with *HOG'S LARD!* Although she never left – or cleaned – her home in London's Clerkenwell district, none of this can have done her any harm as she lived to be *116!*

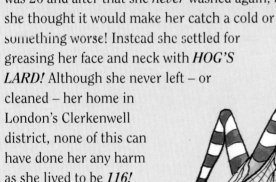

Painting the town red – and white!

The *New York Times* reported in 1879 that a young woman going to a ball used a paintbrush and a lot of *RED AND WHITE PAINT* to give the impression she was wearing fashionable striped stockings!

Don't look so surprised!

A thousand years ago the court ladies of ancient Japan used to shave off their eyebrows and then *PAINT* false ones on half-way up their foreheads!

For that schoolgirl complexion ...

To achieve a fashionably pale look, the ladies of medieval Europe sometimes applied *LEECHES* to drain off the blood from their faces. In the 19th century, before lipstick became 'respectable', women were told to bite their lips HARD to make them redder! Ladies with wrinkles were advised to get rid of them by sleeping with slices of *RAW BEEF* wrapped round their faces – a bit messy on the pillow!

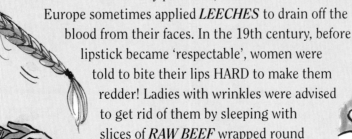

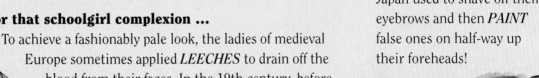

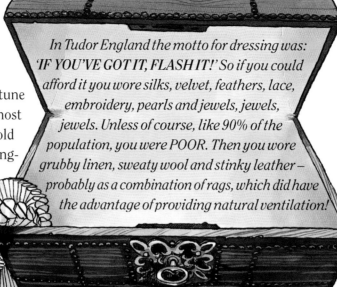

In Tudor England the motto for dressing was: *'IF YOU'VE GOT IT, FLASH IT!'* So if you could afford it you wore silks, velvet, feathers, lace, embroidery, pearls and jewels, jewels, jewels. Unless of course, like 90% of the population, you were POOR. Then you wore grubby linen, sweaty wool and stinky leather – probably as a combination of rags, which did have the advantage of providing natural ventilation!

Buy now, pay later!

Wealthy courtiers spent a fortune on clothes. A noble family's most valuable possession was its gold and silver plate, such as serving-dishes and candlesticks, which together might be worth £1,000. But the Earl of Leicester paid £543 for seven doublets (jackets) and two cloaks! Sir Walter Raleigh paid £30 for a hat-band decorated with pearls. A single African ostrich feather was worth *FIVE DAYS'* wages for a labourer – even before shop-keepers put their profit on! All of this meant good business for tailors – providing they didn't go broke waiting to be paid. Only people with an income of over £3,000 a year were supposed to be able to buy clothes on credit – but many rich people only paid their bills once a year!

The TRENDY Tudors

Don't rush it or you'll crush it

Around 1540 women began to wear a sort of cone of wooden or wire rings called a farthingale under the skirt, which made it fall in long, uncreased folds. Later it got less like a cone and more like a barrel, until some were as much as *1.2 METRES* across. How did women sit down? *Very* slowly!

High and mighty

Fashion was set by the court. The idea was to look bigger, brighter or grander than ordinary people. People like judges, mayors, priests – *and teachers!* – wore gowns made of up to *11 METRES* of cloth, to make them look broad-shouldered. Henry VIII (1509–47) *was* broad-shouldered, as well as 1.88 metres tall (most men were about 1.68 m tall). By the time he was 50 he was broad *EVERYWHERE* – 1.37 m around the waist!

Neck-ruffs grew to be *23 CENTIMETRES* deep. What made this possible was the invention of starch, using flour, which made the ruff stick out. If you got caught in the rain the whole thing collapsed and streaked your doublet with runny pastry-mix!

Breeches were worn baggy and to just above the knee. To make them stand out, they were often stuffed with bombast – a mixture of cotton, or even *bran*. (VERY embarrassing if they got torn open and leaked!)

What shall I wear today?

By the 1590s, Elizabeth I (1558–1603) owned 102 French gowns, 100 loose gowns, 67 round gowns, 99 robes, 127 cloaks, 85 doublets, 125 petticoats, 126 kirtles (under-skirts) and 56 skirts. She died owning about *3,000* garments! The new queen, Anne of Denmark, wouldn't wear second-hand clothes – until she saw them, and had them altered to fit her.

Smile, please!

When she was in her 60s, Elizabeth I's teeth were in a bad way. According to a German visitor, they were quite *BLACK* as a result of eating too many sweets. According to the French ambassador, they were *YELLOW* – more so on one side than the other – but most of them were *MISSING* anyway. So it was difficult to understand what she was saying. (Or maybe she'd forgotten her French by then!)

Hand *OUT* of glove

Elizabeth I liked expensive, embroidered gloves. By pulling them on and off all the time, she could make sure everybody noticed her long, slender fingers! Gloves were often perfumed. Once doused in perfume, they never lost the smell.

DIAMONDS & DO££AR$

Jewel carriageway
Medieval people believed that jewels could protect them from danger, especially when they were travelling! *DIAMONDS* were supposed to guard against ghosts and *SAPPHIRES* against snake-bites. *RUBIES* were supposed to prevent bad dreams from coming true. Perhaps they overlooked the fact that wearing all those jewels would make you much more likely to be robbed!

What am I bid for this *FAKE*?
The Duchess of Windsor's jewellery, auctioned after her death in 1987, raised *£31,380,197*. One necklace of *ARTIFICIAL* pearls and *FAKE* diamonds fetched *£30,000* – just because it had belonged to her!

Don't look cheap!
The most expensive garment ever was a wedding-dress made in France in 1989. Embroidered with *DIAMONDS* mounted on *PLATINUM*, it was valued at *$7.3 MILLION!*

   The most expensive fabric on regular sale is a *vicuna* (llama wool) cloth manufactured in Osaka, Japan. It is priced at a *MILLION YEN* a metre – roughly £5,000!

Star quality
In the 1944 film *Lady in the Dark*, American dancer Ginger Rogers wore a mink and sequin dress which cost $35,000 – *5%* of the cost of the entire film!

Pearly Queen
Queen Alexandra, wife of Edward VII, set a fashion for high *choker* collars of pearl necklaces. She wore them to cover an operation scar on her throat!

A bargain at $200,000!
The world's largest *PEARL* weighs *6.37 KILOS!* It was found in the shell of a giant clam in the Philippines in 1934. In 1980 it was auctioned in San Francisco for $200,000. Four years later, experts valued it at *$42 MILLION!*

It's the tops!
The Cullinan Diamond, found in South Africa in 1905, weighed 3,106 carats (about *650 GRAMS*) and was the size of a baseball. It was given to King Edward VII (1901–10) to become part of the British Crown Jewels. A Dutch expert was called in to cut it. After the first cut he fainted! When he came round he was told it had been perfect. He fainted again! The Cullinan was eventually cut into 106 polished stones. The largest – *530.2 CARATS* – is called the 'Star of Africa' and is set in the royal sceptre. Its value can only be guessed – *$100 MILLION* might be a fair starting bid!

KIDS' STUFF

Who are you trying to fool?

Until the 18th century boys AND girls wore dresses up to the age of six. Boys were thought more precious than girls and so more likely to be harmed by *EVIL SPIRITS!* Dress boys like girls and the spirits would be fooled!

A uniform style

The first clothes specially for children were the uniforms of the 'Blue Coat' charity schools. Blue was the cheapest dye. Yellow was chosen for their stockings as it was supposed to ward off *RATS!*

Knickerbocker glory!

In 1886, Frances Hodgson Burnett wrote *Little Lord Fauntleroy*. It sold a million copies in English alone. Its great popularity meant LOTS of boys in Britain and America were dressed like the book's hero – in a knickerbocker suit of dark *VELVET,* a *SILK* sash and shirt with a *LACE* collar and cuffs!

Tom thumbs

Before the 19th century children were dressed as miniature adults, instead of having clothes specially designed for them. Elizabeth I was wearing corsets at the age of *three!* Occasionally the flow of fashion worked in reverse – trousers began as a fashion for *BOYS,* not men!

Mini-millionairess

Born in 1928, curly-headed Shirley Temple began in films when she was four and was Hollywood's top star four years running, from 1935 to 1938 – a record never equalled before or since. She became the youngest person ever to win an Oscar and the youngest to appear on the cover of *Time* magazine or in *Who's Who*. Ten firms paid her *$1,000* a week for permission to make and sell 'Shirley Temple' dresses, coats, hats, shoes, underwear, hair ribbons, dolls, soap, books, toys and cereal bowls. In 1933 she was the seventh highest-paid person in the USA. By the time she retired as a teenager she had made over *$4,000,000*.

17th- and 18th-century French aristocrats spent lots of time at court and so had to keep up with fashion-conscious kings and queens. A man's suit might have up to 150 metres of ribbon on it! French courtiers rarely went outdoors, but English aristocrats loved riding and hunting, so their clothes were much plainer!

PLAIN & *Fancy*

Not spaghetti! – macaroni!

In 1764 a group of young English show-offs who had all been to Italy founded the Macaroni Club – to let everyone know they had all been to Italy! They wore *TIGHT-CUT* clothes covered with expensive *LACES*, *BOWS*, *TASSELS* and *RIBBONS,* and even carried handbags (to stop their watches or snuff-boxes making ugly bulges in their pockets!) On top of all this a Macaroni wore a wig weighing over *2 KILOS* – with a tiny hat perched on that!

Look at it *this* way!

The farthingale fell out of fashion around 1625. About 1710 the idea of skirt-support came back and women began to wear hoops of cane and canvas that were flat and wide – about *2 METRES* wide! Sideways on, women looked very slim. Frontways on, they looked like a walking *FIREPLACE!* Hooped skirts were *great* for showing off beautiful woven silks, but getting through doorways and out of carriages was an obvious problem! Hinged hoops came in around 1760 to make this easier.

Tartan terror

In 1745 the Highlanders of Scotland rose in rebellion to put Bonnie Prince Charlie on the throne. After their rising was crushed, Parliament banned the wearing of *KILTS*, *PLAIDS* and *TREWS* as weapons of war!

Take cover!

Umbrellas were introduced from France to England in the 18th century. The first users were jostled and hissed in the streets by coachmen who thought the new invention would do them out of fares! By the 1850s Londoners could buy more than *100* different designs with built-in *SWORDS*, *WHISTLES* and *LIGHTNING-CONDUCTORS*. To protect herself against assassins, Queen Victoria carried a parasol that was lined with *CHAIN MAIL!*

Jack Tar

Sailors in the 18th-century Royal Navy often wore their hair plaited into a *pigtail* which was then coated in *TAR!* They also wore hats, and sometimes shirts, of leather '*jacked*' (coated) with tar to make them waterproof – hence the nickname '*Jack Tar*' for a sailor!

Patched-up

Smallpox, which was widespread at the time, left deep scars on the face. Both men and women covered them with lots of patches in fancy shapes like *STARS* and *CRESCENT MOONS*.

Yankee Doodle

When British soldiers fought against American '*Yankee*' rebels during the War of Independence, they made up a song about the rebel army because the rebels didn't have proper uniforms:
'Yankee Doodle came to town
Riding on a pony,
Stuck a feather in his hat
And called it Macaroni!'

Show a leg!

As men's coats became shorter and long boots became unfashionable, more and more of the leg was revealed. Men with *SKINNY LEGS* were afraid of looking like wimps and some took to wearing *FALSE CALVES*. Unfortunately these were very easy to detect – unless you wore at least *THREE PAIRS* of stockings on top of them!

Uniform progress

When grenades came into use after 1700, soldiers trying to throw them kept knocking off their *BROAD-BRIMMED HATS!* A tall, rimless, conical hat was soon adopted for grenade-throwers, who became known as '*grenadiers*'. As the soldiers were usually picked for their height (so they could throw further), their hats got taller and taller to make them look even more imposing! Officers took to tying the tails of their *LONG WIGS* together at the back of their necks to stop them blowing in front of their faces during a battle! The ends were tucked into a *BLACK CLOTH PURSE*, so the style became known as a *bag-wig*. This style was so practical that it was soon copied by civilians!

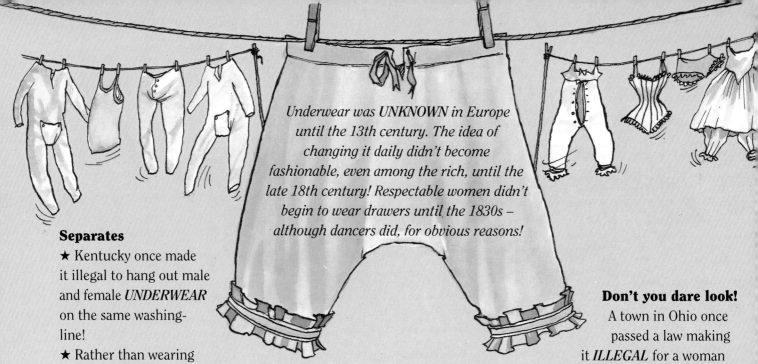

Underwear was UNKNOWN in Europe until the 13th century. The idea of changing it daily didn't become fashionable, even among the rich, until the late 18th century! Respectable women didn't begin to wear drawers until the 1830s – although dancers did, for obvious reasons!

Separates

★ Kentucky once made it illegal to hang out male and female *UNDERWEAR* on the same washing-line!

★ Rather than wearing *UNDERPANTS*, poor men had a cotton lining sewn in their trousers. It was taken out weekly for washing!

Knickers!

Don't you dare look!

A town in Ohio once passed a law making it *ILLEGAL* for a woman to undress in front of a man's picture!

Breathe in!

The 16th-century fashion for long, slim waists led to the invention of tight corsets, first made of *WOOD*, then of *METAL* and then of more pliable *WHALEBONE!* Corsets of varying lengths and styles remained in fashion until the 1790s and were re-introduced in the 1830s. In the 1840s and 1850s many MEN wore corsets to give them an upright 'military' figure, especially when riding! Army officers went on wearing them after the fashion faded among civilians. Corsets were at their tightest in the 1880s and 1890s. With tight lacing, a 55-centimetre waist could be reduced to *48 cm!* Doctors protested that young girls were inflicting serious damage on their insides by lacing their bodies in so tightly. *FAINTING FITS* and *GIDDINESS* were common. Tight corsets were gradually given up as young women wanted to take part in active sports like cycling and tennis and to do new dances like the '*cakewalk*' and '*tango*'. But even uncorseted ladies wore layers of heavy undergarments. In 1888 the radical 'Rational Dress Society' recommended that women should wear *not more than* 7 lb (*3.2 KILOS*) of underclothes!

Keep it clean!
A 17th-century method
for washing underclothes:
1 Trample them in cold water.
(Heating water costs money!)
2 Wring them out and spread
them on a lawn or hedge to dry.
3 For that extra-white finish, bleach
them with stale (it *must* be *stale*) URINE!
WITH REAL AMMONIA! (Waste not, want not!)

Shhhh!

Victorians were so *EMBARRASSED* by the idea
of undergarments that they referred to them as
'*underpinnings*', '*indescribables*', '*unmentionables*'
and '*unwhisperables*'! The 'all-in-one' vest and pants
garments for men were known as '*combinations*' in
Britain and '*union suits*' in the USA. The word '*knickers*'
is short for '*knickerbockers*'. The 19th-century American
writer Washington Irving wrote a *History of New York*
under the name Diedrich Knickerbocker, pretending
to be a descendant of Dutch settlers who founded New
York as 'New Amsterdam'. English cartoonist George
Cruikshank illustrated the book with pictures of
Dutchmen in *BAGGY BREECHES* gathered at the
knee. They became known as 'knickerbockers'!

Posh wash

In Victorian times ordinary people had a washday
every week. But the rich had a washday once a month
or even once every three months. This showed they
had so many clothes that they didn't need to keep
washing them! An 1837 guide-book for brides said
that a young woman should have a 'bottom drawer'
of **96** *CHEMISES*, **48** *NIGHTIES* and **48** *PETTICOATS*.
(No mention of knickers!) Another sign of
being posh was having underwear that did
up at the *BACK* rather than the front.
This meant you could afford to employ
a maid to dress you!

See-through

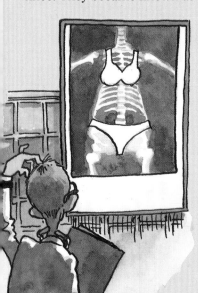

X-rays were discovered
in 1895. Some people
didn't understand how
they'd be used. Almost
immediately, an English
manufacturer began
to promote a range of
'*X-RAY PROOF*' ladies'
underwear!

Isn't it time you got some?

As recently as 1946 a survey
revealed *ONE IN SEVEN*
Englishmen did *not* own
a pair of underpants! (Shirts
were then made with very full
'tails' which could be wrapped
around like a sort of nappy!)

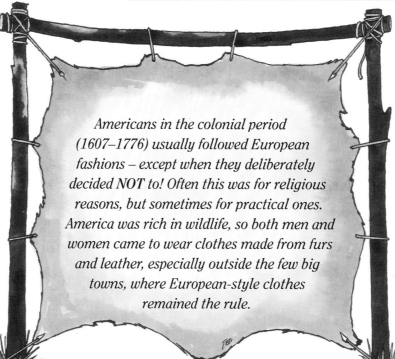

Americans in the colonial period (1607–1776) usually followed European fashions – except when they deliberately decided NOT to! Often this was for religious reasons, but sometimes for practical ones. America was rich in wildlife, so both men and women came to wear clothes made from furs and leather, especially outside the few big towns, where European-style clothes remained the rule.

FRONTIER FASHIONS

Do-it-yourself

As a rule, the RICHER they were, the more European the colonists stayed, because they could afford to pay for imports shipped all the way across the Atlantic, or to have imitations made up by scarce, skilled dressmakers. No one thought to bring a *SPINNING-WHEEL* or a *LOOM* to the colonies until the 1670s. After that, frontier people began to make their own '*homespun*' cloth out of locally grown flax and wool. They coloured it with dyes made from local plants.

If it moves ... wear it!

On the frontier, game was so plentiful that *LEATHER* and *FURS* were much cheaper than woven cloth, as well as being harder-wearing. Furs were used to line cloaks and to make mittens and muffs for winter. Thigh-high boots protected cloth breeches from tearing in dense forest. Jerkins made of leather could stop an arrow! Such tough garments could be passed down from one generation to another. (Phew!!!)

Learning from the locals

Frontier hunters adopted the native Americans' baggy, *buckskin* shirt and leggings – tough, but soft and comfortable. *Fringes* were added as they let the water run out faster when the garments were soaked. They could also be pulled off to make repairs with. And they helped camouflage the outline of the body when out hunting. *Moccasins* made it easier to stalk game silently than heavy boots did. In winter they could be lined with *BUFFALO HAIR* or *MOSS*.

When did you last change your clothes?

The Quakers settled in Pennsylvania in the 1680s. Their standard dress followed the normal fashions of the period – MINUS the ribbons, lace and other fripperies. They then stopped following fashion altogether, and within 50 years the way they dressed was thought of as 'Quaker style'. By then the Amish, from Germany, had also settled in America to follow their religion in freedom. Like the Quakers, they dropped out of the fashion race. Nowadays there are about 50 Amish communities in the USA, where men still wear broad-brimmed hats, shirts without ties and jackets without lapels. Moustaches are banned, but hair is worn long at the sides and married men MUST have a beard! The women wear bonnets, long, full dresses, shawls and black stockings. No jewellery is worn and all clothes are fastened with hooks and eyes or strings rather than buttons!

Bad news for beavers

Some time around 1680, somebody realised that as beavers spend half their lives in water without shrinking, they must have pretty *WATERPROOF FUR!* This brilliant thought led to the idea of using beaver fur to make felt for hats, and the discovery that broad-brimmed beaver-felt hats could stand *endless* downpours without losing their shape. Europeans went crazy for the idea and Canada got a great new business. GOOD NEWS for hunters –
BAD NEWS for beavers!

Sleep on it!

The *best* beaver pelts were prepared by the wives of the hunters. They chewed them to make them soft and then slept on them for a *YEAR* to wear off the coarse reddish hairs and expose the fine grey ones underneath!

The natural look I

France's King Louis XVI (1774–93) and his courtiers, who all wore powdered wigs, were astonished when the American diplomat Benjamin Franklin came to court – wearing *HIS OWN HAIR!* Within a few years wigs, like any sign of the old aristocracy, were OUT. Anyone who wanted to keep their heads on their shoulders kept their own hair on their heads!

Read all about it!

Fashions changed so fast that the first fashion magazines were published, in Paris (1785) and London (1794), to help people keep up. Before that they had relied on travelling salesmen who used *SCALE-MODEL DOLLS* to demonstrate the latest styles.

In 1776 the Americans had a revolution to change their government. In 1789 the French had a revolution which soon began to change EVERYTHING – including fashion. As more and more aristocrats got sent to the guillotine, it became sensible not to look anything like one! Silks, wigs and perfumes were OUT – crumpled clothes, and greasy hair were IN.

YOU'RE REVOLTING

The natural look II

Women got away from the artificial court fashions of the past by dumping wigs, hoops, brocades, fans and high-heeled silk slippers. Instead they wore – *ALMOST NOTHING!* Long, low-cut, high-waisted gowns in creamy, almost see-through, muslin hung on them like the draped garments on a Greek statue. But wearing what you *think* the Greeks wore (ancient Greek women would have thought such dresses quite *indecent*) does not mean you have a Greek climate! So they shivered. Some made things even worse by damping their dresses to make them cling more! The sensible ones wrapped up in warm, lightweight cashmere shawls, which suddenly became *the* fashion accessory!

A shade too heavy

In 1793 the French General Beuronville was captured and imprisoned by the Austrians. He tried to escape by jumping off a 12-metre wall, using one of the newfangled *UMBRELLAS* as a parachute. Unfortunately he was much too heavy for it, broke his leg on landing and was immediately recaptured! The first hot-air balloon flights were also made during this period – the balloonists regularly carried umbrellas to use as *PARACHUTES*.

On guard!

During the French Revolution, instead of swords, civilians took to carrying walking-canes with swords *inside* them!

A breach of good manners

Aristocratic French men had all worn silk breeches – *culottes* – while peasants and workers wore *TROUSERS*. Revolutionaries were therefore called 'sansculottes' – 'without breeches'! Tsar Alexander I of Russia, who was violently opposed to the French Revolution, thought anyone wearing trousers must be plotting to overthrow his throne. In 1807 he ordered his troops to stop all carriages and inspect their male passengers. Anyone in trousers had them cut off at the knees on the spot!

The boys in blue

Britain's first police force was founded in London in 1829. To reassure people that they were *not* soldiers who would be used to bully them into good behaviour, the new police wore *BLUE* uniforms. (Soldiers wore *RED*.) In fact almost all the new policemen *were* ex-soldiers! They wore their uniforms off duty as well as on, so people knew they were about and were on their *best* behaviour!

Meltdown!

In 1823 Charles Macintosh of Glasgow took out a patent for a cloth with a layer of rubber to make coats which really were *RAINPROOF.* Unfortunately they were *VERY SMELLY* and passengers inside coaches often refused to let people in if they were wearing them. They also melted in hot weather! By 1850 a Lancashire firm had learned how to make a coat that sold as 'FFO' – Free From Odour!

The Beau

George 'Beau' Brummell (1778–1840) started off quite sensible and ended up quite *MAD!* He really did revolutionize men's clothing and thanks to him England replaced France as the pace-setter for fashion – even for the *French.* Instead of embroidered silk coats, he wore plain, dark woollen jackets, cut to hug his handsome figure. Instead of fussy, frilly, lace-fringed shirts, he wore plain, white, starched linen with a crisp, perfectly folded cravat. Instead of relying on perfumes to cover up the *SMELL* from his linen and himself, he changed his shirts *EVERY DAY* and spent *two hours* every morning scrubbing himself clean before he even started to dress – which took another *three hours!* The Prince of Wales copied Brummell slavishly. On one occasion he *BURST INTO TEARS* when Brummell told him his jacket didn't fit properly!

When Brummell wanted to go out, he had a sedan chair brought right *INSIDE HIS HOUSE* so that he wouldn't get the soles of his boots dirty (yes, they were polished, too!) by actually *walking* on the pavement. When he was at a party, he wouldn't turn his head to speak to people in case it creased his cravat! For a while every top London maker of shirts, boots, cravats and jackets was happy to dress the 'Beau' on *credit* because he was the best possible advertising they could get. But in the end their patience wore out. Brummell fled to France, where he died in an asylum.

English Eccentrics

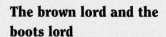

Green man of Brighton

Henry Cope lived at the same time as Brummell. *Everything* he wore was *GREEN!* So was his furniture! He ate only green fruit and vegetables. Eventually, he went mad too.

The brown lord and the boots lord

The Fourth Earl of Harrington (same period!) liked *BROWN!* He drove a brown carriage and dressed his servants in brown uniforms. He didn't trust his tailor to cut the cloth for his jackets properly, so he did it himself. He also had a different *SNUFF-BOX* for *every day of the year.*

The Eighth Earl of Bridgewater had a different pair of *BOOTS* for each day of the year! He kept *15* pet dogs, which he dressed in the current fashion – *complete* with boots! They ate at his table unless they had bad manners, when they had to go to the servants' hall and wear servants' clothes!

Shady stuff

The Mexican '*sombrero*' originated in Spain and takes its name from the Spanish '*sombra*', or shade. One of the most popular sun-hats is the *panama* – which was first made in *ECUADOR!*

TOP THAT!

Don't do it again!

The 'top hat' was first worn on 15 January 1797 by John Hetherington, a London hat-maker. It caused such a sensation that four women *FAINTED* and a small boy had his arm broken in the crowd that gathered to look at it!

Hetherington was arrested and in court the judge made him swear not to wear it again – or face a fine of £500. Despite this, the '*topper*' became the standard high-fashion hat for men in the 19th century.

Deertective

Arthur Conan Doyle intended his creation Sherlock Holmes to seem *VERY WEIRD* by having this London-based detective wear a '*deerstalker*' hat worn by hunters. Perhaps it was supposed to suggest that Holmes tracked criminals like a dedicated hunter?

Bowled over!

In the 19th century, a Mr William Coke asked a hatter to design something more practical for hunting than a top hat. They came up with a low, round hat, made of *RABBIT FUR* hardened with a varnish called '*shellac*'. As they were later made by a firm called Bowler they are now known as *bowler hats*, but when they were invented they were called '*billycocks*' – after William Coke. He tested the first one by jumping on it *TWICE!* Americans call the same hat a '*derby*' because American visitors to England first saw it at the Derby, a famous horse-race.

Fighting talk

'*At the drop of a hat*' nowadays means 'immediately'. The expression comes from an American frontier custom of dropping a hat as a signal for a *FIGHT* to begin!

Looks a bit fishy to me...

Porters at London's Billingsgate fish market wore flat-topped hats which let them balance a *100 kilo* box of wet fish on their heads! Each hat was made out of 2 kilos of leather, 10 metres of waxed thread and 400 brass rivets!

Crinolines

The Regency fashion for light, flowing dresses was followed by an extreme reaction in which women seemed to want to cover up *everything!* Even the face itself was often covered with a veil and the hands with lace mittens. The natural shape of the body was disguised and distorted with corsets and petticoats and stuffed sleeves. One good thing though – making all those complicated clothes provided work for **340,000** women in Britain alone!

Bell of the ball

The fashionable dresses of the 1850s wanted to make women look like handbells. The bell-shaped outline was achieved by piling on layers of petticoats, usually starched and often further stiffened with *HORSE-HAIR*. For a formal occasion, like a ball, a woman might need to wear as many as *16* petticoats! In winter extra layers of flannel, or petticoats stuffed with eider-down, might be worn for warmth. Then, in 1856, came the crinoline – a light cage of hoops and tapes, rather like a complicated version of a lamp-shade frame. From then on the petticoats weren't needed.

A growth industry

The cheapest crinolines were made of *split cane*, the best of *watch-spring steel*. There were even experimental models made of *rubber*, inflated with a *FOOT-PUMP* and sold as an '*air tube dress extender*'! The largest styles were *6 METRES* in circumference. The biggest manufacturer of crinolines, Thomson's of Cheapside in London, employed a labour force of 1,000 women and turned out 4,000 a day. When it was first invented, Queen Victoria called the crinoline 'indelicate, expensive, hideous and dangerous'. Five years later she was wearing one herself!

Bustle without hustle

Within ten years the crinoline was OUT – mainly because even servants and peasants were wearing them. The new fashion was the '*crinolette*' or bustle, a sort of half-crinoline worn at the back. Getting through doors was much easier – but *sitting down* was still tricky! Hi-tech bustles had a complicated spring mechanism which folded up as you sat down, then whizzed back into place as you stood up. Cheap bustles were made from almost anything light-weight, even *OLD NEWSPAPERS*. In Chester, a lady wearing a bustle stuffed with *BRAN* was attacked by a donkey who thought he'd have it for lunch! It now became fashionable to have a *very* straight back. You could make your back look straighter by having your bustle stick out at right-angles, rather than sloping away gently. It was said that a *TEA-TRAY* could be balanced on the most extreme examples!

& Bustles

A matter of life and death

In the home or, worse still, in a factory, the crinoline was a *MENACE!* In 1860 Courtaulds – which made silks for crinolines – banned them from their factory after a series of horrific accidents in which women wearing crinolines had been dragged into moving machines. For a woman in a crinoline, the open coal fire which burned in almost every room of a normal house was a real hazard. Just brushing against it could be *FATAL*, as metres of material could go up in flames before the wire frame underneath could be ripped off!

But the crinoline could also be a *LIFE-SAVER!* In 1862 a young woman tried to kill herself by jumping off the Clifton suspension bridge in Bristol and floated down to safety – *80 METRES* below! In the same year, a party of young American ladies were rescued from a boating accident, thanks to crinolines which trapped air beneath them and acted as enormous *LIFE-BELTS!*

Not exactly easy-care

Another problem with crinolines was keeping them clean. Wearing them to balls was a hazard. Women had to avoid men treading on them with their big boots! Maids stitched absorbent under-arm pads to the dresses to soak up sweat. But usually cleaning meant taking the whole dress apart to wash every piece by hand!

The original 501s

Levis are named after their inventor, Levi Strauss. He set up as a store-keeper and found that miners were wearing out a pair of trousers every three weeks. In 1850 he began to make the first 'jeans', using canvas sail-cloth. They

sold for *$13.50* a *DOZEN PAIRS!* Later he switched to the blue cloth known as 'denim' because it was made in Nimes, France ('de Nimes' – from Nimes).

In the 1870s he made the trousers even tougher by adding copper rivets to the pockets; this enabled miners to cram more samples into them.

In 1899 a pair of Levis was used in Arizona to make a temporary coupling when a train broke down. The jeans hauled seven coaches over 16 km to the next station!

WAY OUT WEST

How to look like a REAL cowboy:
★ *Ride behind the herd all day and get covered with dust.*
★ *Fall in **every** muddy river you cross.*
★ *Sit **real close** to a smoky camp-fire every night.*
★ *Don't take off **anything** during the **four-month** cattle-drive. You will then **look** like a REAL cowboy and **smell** like one too!*

Even the cows must have been wearing them!

By 1906 the Stetson Hat Company was employing 3,500 people to turn out 2 million hats a year!

Wet, wet, wet

In rainy weather cowboys' canvas **ankle-length 'slicker' coats** were water-proofed with linseed oil. The summer version was called a 'duster', as it kept off the dust when they rode 'drag' at the back of the herd.

What cowboys *should* have put in their saddle-bags

Spare shirt, socks, underwear, soap, towel, comb, razor …

What cowboys *did* put in their saddlebags

Cartridges, mouth-organ, tobacco, coffee-beans, playing-cards …

How's the hat?

Cowboys were very proud of their hats and would pay up to $20 for them, almost a month's wages and twice the price of a pair of boots.

Cowboys used their hats for
★ signalling to each other when they were too far apart to shout
★ fanning their camp-fires
★ carrying water to sick calves
★ wearing!

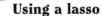

Using a lasso
Rule 1 Throw the end with the noose in it.
Rule 2 *DON'T* throw the other end!

Gloves – *remember...* only cissies wore gloves. You could tell the hands of a real tough hombre by
★ the *CACTUS-SPINES* sticking out of them
★ the *ROPE-BURNS* on the palms
★ the *MISSING FINGERS!*

A wide-brimmed hat kept off the sun's glare in summer and rain or snow in winter. **Shaggy hair** helped too.

The bright bandana was worn to keep the trail-dust out of the cowboy's mouth. It was also used as a towel, a tourniquet – or a sling! In winter it could be tied over the hat to pull it down on the ears.

Jeans were too tight for cowboys on horseback to reach into their pockets, so **waistcoats** were worn to hold tobacco or a pocket-knife.

Sacred saddles
A cowboy's saddle was his most expensive item of equipment, costing about $45 – or *TWO MONTHS' SALARY*. In 1914 Joe C. Miller of the 101 Ranch in Oklahoma paid *$10,000* for a saddle decorated with *166 DIAMONDS, 120 SAPPHIRES, 17 RUBIES* and *7 KILOS* of *SILVER AND GOLD!*

The pointed toes of a cowboy's **boots** helped get them in the stirrups on a frisky horse. Their high heels held him steady while standing up in the stirrups, or digging into the ground when roping a steer.

Cowboys who could afford them wore **over-trousers** called **'chaps'** to protect against cactus and thorns. Made of tanned leather, or fur with the hide left on for extra warmth, these were backless to make them lighter.

(39)

Until Japanese people began to wear Western-style clothes late in the 19th century, the way they dressed told people how IMPORTANT they were and therefore how they should be spoken to! There were rules for how everyone should dress. Nowadays everyone wears much the same clothes, and Japanese people exchange NAME CARDS so that they can tell who is the most senior!

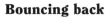

Bouncing back

Sumo wrestlers use a sticky hair oil to hold their *TOP-KNOTS* in place while they're fighting. The top-knot helps to protect the skull if a wrestler gets dropped on his head!

WAY OUT EAST

Samurai style

Samurai warriors had the right to *KILL ON THE SPOT* anyone who wasn't suffficiently polite to them! Fortunately, it was fairly easy to spot a samurai! He always had *TWO SWORDS* sticking out of his waistband. The *long one* was for fighting. The *short one* was for cutting off the heads of dead enemies – or for killing himself if he thought he was going to be on the losing side in a battle!

Samurai also had a *very distinctive* hair-style. The top of the head was *SHAVED* as far back as the crown. The sides were grown long, then gathered into a *PONY-TAIL*. This was stiffened with a type of hair oil and bound up into a stick shape, which was then twisted so that it *POINTED FORWARD* over the bald part!

Court out

12th-century ladies at court admired pale complexions, so they stayed IN when the sun came OUT! They grew their hair so LONG they could stand on it! And as white teeth reminded people of dogs or rats, they used *RICE-VINEGAR* and *IRON FILINGS* to coat their teeth a nice shiny black!

Take it easy...

For *special occasions*, ladies wore brightly coloured silk kimonos – up to *12* of them, one on top of another! This created a rainbow of shades at the wrists and down the front where they overlapped. It looked lovely – the problem was being able to *MOVE* under all that! This sort of costume was worn by Miss Owada when she married the Crown Prince of Japan in 1993. It weighed *30 KILOS* and cost *£300,000!*

All change!

In the 1870s, Japan's government decided to modernise the country by adopting Western customs. This included changing people's appearance! The Emperor started wearing Western-style *MILITARY UNIFORMS*. The Empress GAVE UP blackening her teeth! Samurai were ordered to CUT OFF their top-knots and STOP carrying swords.

Most people couldn't afford whole sets of expensive imported Western clothes. So they bought what they could! Western visitors at that time were confused to see Japanese wearing graceful kimonos with items like *TOP HATS* and *PLIMSOLLS!*

Have you been biting your nails again?

Most Japanese men wear dark blue or grey suits. But Mafia-type gangsters, called *yakuza*, model their clothes on Chicago gangsters of the 1920s – chalk-stripe suits with big lapels, black and white shoes and bright wide ties. Underneath, many are *TATTOOED* all over. They wear flashy jewellery too – including *dazzling* gold teeth! Some yazuka also have *MISSING FINGER-TIPS!* This is because when a junior gangster makes a mess of a job, he may *CHOP OFF* one of his finger-joints by way of apologising to his boss!

I've got designs on you!

But is it WORTH it?

Everyone thinks the French invented fashion. Just to make the point, really swanky fashions have a fancy-sounding French name – '*haute couture*' – which just means 'high-sewing', actually. Of course, Paris *was* the birth-place of modern fashion. And there *have* been dozens of famous French designers. But the true inventor of 'haute couture' was an *ENGLISHMAN,* Charles Worth (1825–95). In the 1850s Worth had a GREAT IDEA which, *amazingly*, no one had thought of before – why not persuade customers to buy dresses by showing them how good they could look when someone was actually wearing them? In other words, he invented the *MODEL.* Interestingly, the first models were chosen because they were *not* particularly good-looking. After all, Worth was trying to sell *dresses,* not models!

Loosen up!

Frenchman Paul Poiret (1879–1944) told women to throw out their corsets and petticoats and try out *BAGGY PANTS* like Aladdin's, or relax in a Japanese kimono. But around 1908 he introduced the '*hobble skirt*', which was so tight from knee to ankle that it was impossible for a woman to take a stride of more than *20 cm!*

Sweet smell of success

Gabrielle 'Coco' Chanel (1886–1971) noticed during the First World War how unsuitable women's clothes were for doing 'men's jobs', like working with machinery. After the war she produced simple, practical clothes for women, using fabrics like *TWEED, JERSEY* or *CORDUROY,* which had only been worn by men before. Born on 5 August, she believed five was her lucky number and sold a perfume which she called 'Chanel No. 5'. It made her so rich she retired from 1939 to 1954 and then made a successful 'come-back' when she was almost 70!

GOING TO EXTREMES

If you work at dangerous jobs in dangerous places, you need to wear something a bit different. For example, bomb-disposal experts wear jackets that weigh over *24 KILOS* to protect them from explosions!

Mined how you breathe
Miners in ancient Rome wore transparent *BLADDER-SKIN MASKS* to protect them from poisonous dust!

Ace for space
NASA's first space-suit designers visited the Tower of London to examine *HENRY VIII'S ARMOUR*, because its jointing was so snug and skilful. What they came up with by the time of the Apollo VIII mission in 1968 had *17* layers – including one of Teflon, which is now widely used to give cooking pans a non-stick coating!

Polar bare
Suits designed for use at the South Pole, where temperatures plunge to –70°C, and exposed flesh freezes in *25 SECONDS*, have yielded valuable lessons which have been used to design clothing worn in cold stores!

Fearless footwear
Workers on building sites and oil-rigs who handle heavy gear should be grateful for an American invention of the 1930s – boots with *STEEL TOE-CAPS!*

Easily shocked!
In 1866 the London fire brigade adopted new *BRASS HELMETS*. There was no electric wiring in houses then. But brass is an *excellent* conductor of electricity! When houses began to be wired up, the helmet became a hazard. It was dropped in the 1930s.

Finger stinger
From the 1860s onwards, surgeons began to use strong disinfectants to kill germs on their patients. From 1878 *RUBBER GLOVES* became available to protect their own hands.

Hot stuff!
Modern 'snatch suits' enable rescuers to dash in and out of burning aircraft which can reach temperatures of *1,000°C!* Garments coated with aluminium reflect *90%* of the heat they are exposed to.

Magnificent

From 1526 until 1857 India was ruled by a dynasty of emperors called the Mughals. India was famed for its cloth, especially cotton. Calico takes its name from the port of Calicut. Dungarees were originally made from 'dungri', a tough calico. Bandanas are named from a method of dyeing to produce a polka-dot pattern. Cashmere is a mis-spelling of mountainous Kashmir, where goats' hair was woven into light, warm rugs.

So long!

It's a good job India has always made a lot of cloth. A woman's sari needs *at least* 6 metres. The sort of baggy trousers worn in the Punjab take up to 10 metres and a turban can take up to *25 METRES!* The words '*turban*' and '*tulip*' come from the same Persian root.

Canned elephant

As tanks hadn't been invented yet, the Mughal army used armoured *elephants* instead. The armour weighed about *160 KILOS,* and included *SWORDS* which were fitted on to the ends of the elephants' tusks!

British borrowings

Khaki uniforms were first worn by British soldiers in India. '*Khaki*' means mud or dust in Persian. British soldiers also wore puttees, 6-metre strips of cloth, wound tightly round the leg from knee to ankle. '*Puttee*' means bandage in Hindi. Pyjamas were originally lightweight baggy trousers worn at home in hot weather. The famous '*Paisley pattern*' woven at Paisley in Scotland is in fact an INDIAN design based on the *CYPRESS TREE!*

Play the game!

Loose cotton '*polo shirts*' are now worn to relax in. Originally they were designed to wear while playing polo – which was brought to Europe and America from India. Polo began in Central Asia, where steppe nomads used to play with the *HEAD* of a defeated enemy instead of a ball! The tight-fitting breeches worn by polo-players are called *jodhpurs* after the Indian city of Jodhpur.

Oh, dry up!

The British in India found the climate *very* sweaty. One lawyer changed his clothes so often he had 71 pairs of breeches and 81 waistcoats. Victorian ladies wore *RUST-PROOF CORSETS!*

Mughals

Living in luxury

The Mughals lived in *amazing* luxury. Emperor Akbar (1556–1605) had a library of 24,000 books – but he couldn't *read!* Naturally, he was a nifty dresser. He was said to get through 1,000 outfits a year (that's *THREE A DAY*). In fact he probably got a lot of these as gifts and gave them away without even wearing them – but he *did* have 120 suits permanently on stand-by to choose from! Akbar's life-story was written by his friend, Abul Fazl. He used to give *ALL* his clothes away to his servants at the end of every year.

Twinkle, twinkle

At the age of 18, the Maharani of Jodhpur wore so much jewellery that she needed *TWO ATTENDANTS* to help her stand upright. She even wore false eyebrows made of *DIAMONDS*.

Too rich to care

The last ruler of Hyderabad had about *£30 MILLION* in cash and more than that amount in gold and jewels, including ten emeralds, each as big as an egg. After he died, his son went through his father's clothes and found a *162-CARAT* diamond stuffed in the toe of a slipper!

Well, just this once then...

George V (1910–1936) was the only British ruler actually to go to India when it was under British control. In 1911 he went to Delhi to hold a 'durbar', a meeting where all the rajahs and princes could come and accept him as the new emperor of India. There was just one snag. The law forbids the Crown Jewels to leave Britain. As he wouldn't have looked like a king without a crown, all the rajahs and princes chipped in to make him a special one just for the occasion. It had *6,000 DIAMONDS* – more gemstones than any other item in the Crown Jewels. It has only ever been worn that *ONCE*. The king took care to bring the new crown back. So it isn't kept in India but in the Tower of London. (Seems like you *can't* export Crown Jewels, but you *can* import them!)

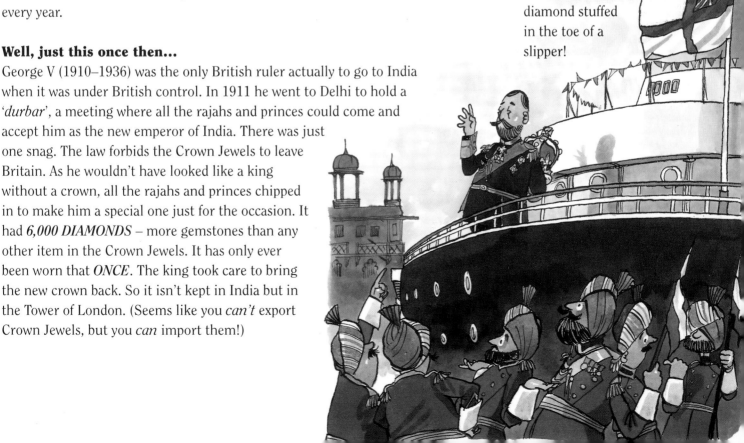

A·R·O·U·N·D 1920

The 1920s and 1930s were a period of revolt and crazes – and some revolting crazes! After the First World War young people wanted to have a good time. They didn't want to go back to the dull, formal clothes of the 1900s. They wanted to dance to jazz music – so GOODBYE to corsets! They wanted to go hiking – so HELLO to shorts! But you still had to wear a hat and gloves, of course!

PLUS FOURS — AND — PYJAMAS

Hanging around – or going up!

A fashion for *immensely* baggy trousers began among rich students at Oxford University. Some '*Oxford bags*' were over **60 cm** round at the bottom and completely hid the feet!

Meanwhile, in the mid-1920s designers decided skirts should be shorter than ever before – but still below the knee! This was *BAD NEWS* if you were a cloth manufacturer, because so much less was needed. But it was *GOOD NEWS* for makers of stockings and shoes, which suddenly became fashion items! British doctors said that short skirts would make women's legs go puffy and chafed. In Italy, bishops banned bare-legged women from going to church. French tennis star Suzanne Lenglen had to wear stockings when she played in front of Queen Mary at Wimbledon – but she did get away with a sleeveless jumper which showed her bare arms!

Fur enough?

Furs were used to trim coats and hats. The fur of leopards and monkeys was especially fashionable. Whole foxes, complete with head and tail, were worn as shoulder-wraps!

Tut, tut!

In 1922 a team of British archaeologists uncovered the tomb of the Egyptian Pharaoh Tutankhamun. This started a craze for ancient Egypt! Designers brought out hats in the shape of a pharaoh's head-dress, and fabrics covered in *PYRAMIDS* or *HIEROGLYPHS*.

Prince of Wales, King of fashion

Britain's dashing young Prince of Wales, son of George V (1910–36), set the style for wealthy young people. *GOLFING* and *SHOOTING* clothes such as *Fair Isle* sweaters, *Argyll* diamond-pattern socks, *plus four* trousers and *brogue* shoes became popular as general casual wear – but only in the country! The prince also had a triangular tie-knot and a chequer-pattern grey flannel cloth named after him!

Every day is Sun-day

The craze for sun-bathing probably came from wanting to look as if you were RICH enough to take a winter holiday in the Mediterranean or Caribbean! So *BEACH-WEAR* became another new area for the fashion industry to cash in on! Rubber swimming caps were available in dozens of different styles and colours. Loose '*beach pyjamas*' were especially popular for women. Some also wore pyjamas instead of evening gowns. And some even went to sleep in them!

Head case

A '*perm*' (permanent wave) hair-do could cost as much as a *MONTH'S* wages for a secretary! But late-20s fashion required young women to wear a close-fitting '*cloche*' hat which completely covered it up!

Is it a boy or a girl?

Many older people thought the fashions of the 20s made girls look like *BOYS!* Women cut their hair short and dressed to look very slim and flat-chested. Some even wore *TROUSERS!* As they also wore lip-stick and heavy eye make-up, it *should* still have been possible to tell the difference!

American style

'*Boxer shorts*' were originally issued to US infantry men as summer underwear. The modern *T-shirt* began life as a newly designed item of underwear for the US Navy around 1890. In the 1920s, US oil and construction companies adapted steel helmets as '*hard hats*'.

Parade-ground uniforms are meant to look smart. Battle-ground uniforms are meant to be practical. Epaulets on jackets were originally there to show badges of rank. Later they were used as a way of making sure back-packs didn't slip off the shoulders! 'Navy-blue' speaks for itself! So does a 'crew cut' hair-style and the 'crew-neck' sweater.

Jump for it!

Pilots were not issued with *parachutes* until the last years of the First World War. Until then if you were shot down, you crashed! During the Second World War, women were keen to have airmen for boyfriends, as silk from damaged parachutes could be made into lovely underwear or even a wedding-dress! Underwear was hard to get because the machinists who made it were occupied in making balloons, kites, tents, sails, flags and life-jackets.

Baa-baa bomber!

During the Second World War, with planes flying as high as *6,000 METRES* on long-range bombing missions, air crew wore sheepskin '*bomber-jackets*'. These remained standard issue until 1949.

FASHION GOES TO WAR

The First World War

Waterproof '*trench coats*' were first worn in the rain-sodden trenches. The 'D'-shaped brass rings on them were originally there to clip on binoculars, map-cases and other equipment. Coats of thick '*duffel*' cloth were designed for sailors keeping watch; their toggle fastenings were easier to do up with *FROZEN FINGERS* than buttons were. In 1915 the first '*ear-protectors*' were introduced for artillery men. Pilots in open-cockpit planes usually relied on clothes lined with fur or camel fleece to keep out the bitter cold, but there were also experiments with electrically-heated flying-suits, gloves and boots.

Make do and mend

In Britain clothes rationing lasted from 1941 until 1952. Tailors were *FORBIDDEN BY LAW* to make trousers with turn-ups, belts, zips or wide bottoms – or for boys under 12 years of age, who had to wear *shorts!* Jackets were not allowed to be double-breasted or to have patch pockets or more than three buttons. Trimmings of any sort were banned on underwear, nightwear or baby clothes. Housewives turned old blankets into coats and curtains into dresses. Woollen garments were unpicked and re-knitted. The cloth used for wrapping *CHEESE* was not rationed and could be made into underwear! *Stockings* were specially difficult to get. Many women painted their legs with make-up or *COFFEE* and got a friend to draw 'seams' down the back with an *EYE-BROW PENCIL*. It was essential to keep out of the rain after this!

Goodbye Paris, hello New York!

Unable to get French fashions during the War, American women turned to New York designers. Americans on holiday went south and bought colourful Latin American styles. Tiny Brazilian singer Carmen Miranda made herself look tall by wearing *THICK-SOLED,* high-heeled shoes and lots of *FRUIT* on her head!

Thanks to Yanks!

Clothes parcels from friends in America introduced the British to jeans, 'sneakers', 'bobby-socks' and tartan-check shirts. The shortage of silk and satin made glamorous white wedding dresses very scarce. Romantic novelist Barbara Cartland bought *100* from the USA and hired them out at £1 a time to women serving in the armed forces.

Stars on stripes

General Eisenhower, commander of the US forces, had a pair of pyjamas with the five stars of a full general on the lapels! British Prime Minister Churchill had a zip-up *'siren suit'* made of purple velvet. These suits let you dress in a minute when an air-raid siren went!

Stitched up

After the war servicemen were 'demobilised' and swapped their uniform for a 'demob suit. These were available in two sizes – *TOO LARGE* and *TOO SMALL!*

From the 1920s to the rise of television Hollywood was the world's 'dream factory'. The 'golden age of cinema' set fashions in clothes, make-up and hairstyles. Because more women than men went to 'the movies', film-makers often put in scenes of weddings, dances, night-clubs and beaches just to increase the fashion interest. But even men slicked back their hair to look like Rudolph Valentino or turned up their coat-collars to look like gangsters.

Smoothing over

Body hair was regarded as so *unattractive* until the late 1960s that hairy-chested men were routinely *SHAVED* before filming. When Jeffrey Hunter played the part of Jesus in *King of Kings* (1961), he was even shaved under the arms!

Secret of success

Marilyn Monroe's 'wiggle' when she walked wasn't natural. She deliberately had the high heel on one of her shoes made *HIGHER* than the other one. Result – wiggle!

Look left!

A photographer once told 1930s film star Claudette Colbert that she looked her best pictured from the LEFT. After that she insisted that cameramen *always* filmed her from that side, and she had film sets built so that she came into shot showing the left side of her face! She even covered the right side of her face with *GREEN GREASEPAINT,* so that if it was ever filmed by accident the scene would have to be done again!

Hooray for Hollywood!

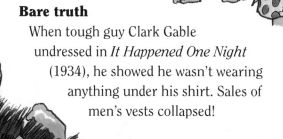

Bare truth

When tough guy Clark Gable undressed in *It Happened One Night* (1934), he showed he wasn't wearing anything under his shirt. Sales of men's vests collapsed!

Stand still a minute!

In *Lady in the Dark* (1944), dancer Ginger Rogers had to dream she was a bride wearing a long wedding dress made with *DOZENS* of metres of material. Unfortunately, the dry ice used to create artificial mist for the 'dreamy' atmosphere soon *SOAKED* into the dress so much that it became impossible for her to move. *Sixteen* wardrobe assistants with ironing boards rushed on stage between every take to iron out the moisture!

Dyeing to look like her

Millions of women bleached their hair with peroxide so they could be platinum blondes like Jean Harlow and Mae West. When auburn-haired Rita Hayworth was popular, they dyed it instead. (So did she!)

Is he *BALD*?

The list of men who wore wigs to cover up their BALDNESS includes Fred Astaire, Humphrey Bogart, Frank Sinatra, Charlton Heston and Burt Reynolds.

Gone with the budget!

Rivalry between studios to turn out ever bigger epics began to mean the amount spent on making a film was looked on as a *guarantee* that it would be great. Sometimes the spending went to amazing lengths. To help make the 2,500 costumes required for the film *Marie Antoinette* (1938), 50 Mexican women were hired full-time just to sew sequins! When Vivien Leigh played 1860s Southern beauty Scarlett O'Hara in *Gone with the Wind* (1939), she was astonished to find that the INSIDES of all her costumes had been hand-stitched, just as they would have been in the 1860s. In the course of the film, she wore over *50* different changes of costume. The largest number of costumes made for a single film was *32,000* for *Quo Vadis* (1951), a historical drama set in ancient Rome.

Can't you keep that dress quiet?

Taffeta, one of the most fashionable dress materials of the 1920s, had to be given up once 'talkies' came in because its loud rustling drowned out the actors' dialogue! *SILENT SATIN* took its place.

Ping Crosby

A film producer decided singer Bing Crosby's large ears stuck out so much they made him look like a sugar bowl! So he ordered the make-up people to stick them to the side of his head with *GUM* – which worked fine until the hot studio lights melted the gum. Then – *PINGGG!!!*

Keeping up appearances

Glamorous Joan Crawford had all her *BACK TEETH* removed to make her cheek bones stand out more! She also had *TWO* facelifts and *MANY* operations to re-arrange her under-sized and widely spaced front teeth. Her face was covered with *freckles,* but these were wiped out in publicity photographs by 'retouching' the negatives. In the 1940s she set a trend for broad, padded shoulders on dresses and jackets.

Crooners and rockers

Singers began to challenge film stars as fashion idols. In the 1940s American music meant 'big bands'. By the early 1950s it meant 'crooners' like Frank Sinatra, Nat King Cole and Johnny Ray, who sang ballads, wore well-tailored suits and had audiences sitting down to listen to them. Then, in the mid-50s came Bill Haley and the Comets, who played 'Rock around the Clock'. Their audiences jumped up and down and danced in the aisles until they were thrown out! In the late 1950s came *ELVIS* – who did the jumping up and

In the 1950s America began to replace Europe as the style-setter, especially for teenagers – perhaps because the 'teenager' was an American invention! For the first time it was OK to look 'casual' and do amazingly daring things – like wearing a shirt flapping OUTSIDE rather than neatly tucked in! Or wearing jeans – without nice straight creases down the front!

ROCK AROUND THE CLOCK

down *himself*. During his act he would throw himself down on his knees – which meant he kept splitting his trousers, until he had them made specially loose, with reinforced seams!

A · R · O · U · N · D
1959

Beatniks

'*Beatniks*' were people who sat in New York wishing they were in Paris! They listened to jazz and worried about the atomic bomb. Men wore roll-neck sweaters, cord trousers, hairy jackets, duffel coats, sandals and beards. Women wore huge, baggy sweaters. They all wore *GLOOMY COLOURS* to show how happy they were!

Teddy Boys

Britain's only original version of teenage style was the '*Teddy Boy*'. The newspapers told readers that 'Teds' were trying to revive the elegance of the England of Edward (Teddy) VII (1901–10) after the drabness of wartime. In fact Teds looked much more like an *American* model – the Mississippi river-boat gambler, who also wore long, draped jackets with *VELVET* collars, *FRILLY-FRONTED* shirts and *TIGHT*, 'drain-pipe' trousers.

The campus look

Millions of American teenagers were still in college when European teenagers had already got jobs and had to wear work clothes or uniforms. Thanks to films and TV, the Europeans could see the campus style and copy it after work – sloppy sweaters, turned-up jeans, shirt-waister dresses, white ankle socks, baseball boots.

Have it in olive green

When US forces left Europe after the war, they sold off *4 MILLION* items! At one auction in Paris in 1947 they sold 9,750 sweaters, 17,310 vests and *20 TONNES* of socks. These war-surplus clothes were still popular in the 1950s.

Grease!

Film stars Marlon Brando and James Dean played screen rebels who rode big, dirty motorbikes and established the rebel uniform of greasy jeans, T-shirts and *BLACK LEATHER JACKETS*.

Space for a change

The 'space race' between the USA and USSR to land an astronaut on the moon inspired fashion which picked up the mood in the mid-60s. In 1964, Paris went wild over designs by Courrèges where the models looked like air-hostesses on a flight to *MARS* – with dresses like surgeons' gowns (much better cut, of course), surgeons' white boots, and hats like helmets!

Star struck

Rock stars' costumes became *outrageous.* American Solomon Burke – 'King of Rock and Soul' – wore a replica of the British Crown Jewels and a 4.5 metre long cape trimmed with *ERMINE*. The Kinks wore *PURPLE VELVET* suits. Mick Jagger of the Rolling Stones wore a white *MINI-DRESS* over white trousers!

> Fashion in the 60s went in three stages. Nothing much changed until 1963. From then until 1967 the 'look' was smart or 'space-age'. Then it all changed again to bells, bangles and beads as the hippy 'flower power' craze spread! Casual clothes continued to win out over formal suits.

the swinging 60s

Making a name for himself

French fashion designer Pierre Cardin went into menswear in 1960 and caused a sensation with the collarless jackets the Beatles made famous world-wide. He also designed neckties of *SUEDE* or *VELVET* which could only be knotted once and then had to be thrown away! Cardin was the first to put his signature on the clothes he designed. By 1965 there were 200 shops in France selling his designs and 700 abroad. Twenty years later you could buy *800* different Cardin products, including skis, dolls, chocolate and toilet seats!

Beatles I

Before the Beatles became famous, they wore the 'rebel uniform' of jeans, T-shirts and black leather jackets. Then their manager took over and they became known as much for their APPEARANCE as for their music. On stage they dressed identically. All four were clean-shaven, with the same doll-like 'mop-top' hair-style, greaseless and combed forward to cover the forehead. They wore odd-looking, collarless 'Beatle jackets' – but with ordinary white shirts and dark knitted ties. Their trousers were cut tight – but still straight, with creases down the front. On their feet they wore elastic-sided 'Beatle boots' with high Cuban heels and squared-off toes!

Don't stand sideways or you'll disappear!

At the age of 16, 'super-model' Lesley Hornby could earn as much in an HOUR posing for a fashion photographer as a teacher could earn in a WEEK! Weighing in at *41 KILOS*, she was soon nicknamed TWIGGY. Guess why?

The thigh's the limit!

Skirts in 1960 were as short as the shortest skirts ever worn in the short-skirted 1920s. By 1965 they were, on average, *20 cm* shorter – which helped to speed up the switch from stockings to tights!

The sky's the limit

Cheap air travel meant fashion 'shoots' in exotic places were easier to set up – models were shown on beaches or striding through jungles, rather than tip-toeing to restaurants or the theatre. With more people travelling by air but taking less luggage, holidaymakers wanted 'easy-care' clothes that would pack easily without creasing badly.

Hipsters and hippies

Hipsters were hip-hugging ultra-tight trousers cut short below the waist. Hippies were INTO Eastern religions and FOR anything that was patched, torn, Indian, Arab, Gypsy, Native American or second-hand. Clothing manufacturers *hated* them!

Beatles II

Five years on and tailored uniforms were OUT. So were neat hair-styles and ties. Each Beatle now dressed *quite differently* – but in the *same style*. Droopy moustaches and shaggy hair were IN. So were open-necked shirts, trousers 'flared' out from the knee, bits of old uniforms, frills, ruffles, satin, velvet, leather, cheesecloth, patchwork and fur. The thing to do was dress up like a pirate – and a bandit and …

THE WHICH WAY 70s

Rock on

With rock concerts held in immense stadiums, performers needed dramatic costumes just to be SEEN by their audiences! Designers used metallic textiles, sequins and rhinestones to sparkle against the lights. Fireworks were also part of the *'Glam rock'* style of Elton John, Alvin Stardust and Gary Glitter.

In the 70s 'fashion' finally gave way to 'fashions'. 'Doing your own thing' meant dressing the way you wanted. Or the way your friends did. Or the way your favourite pop star did. Or the way that would annoy your parents most! And if you thought that the idea of fashion was itself a stupid rip-off – then there was a fashion you could wear to show that, too!

Aren't you exaggerating a bit?

60s trends were carried to extremes – with top coats so LONG they trailed on the ground and shirt collars so BIG they could stretch from shoulder to shoulder! Wide-bottomed trousers, known as *'flares'* or *'loons'*, could completely cover your shoes – unless you wore platform-soled boots which added at least 10 cm to your height!

Now, that's what I call *shorts!*

The mini-skirt simply refused to go away and gave birth to a sort of divided mini-skirt, known as 'hot pants'!

Bigga business!

By the 1970s Italy's clothing industry was worth more than its electrical goods and motor industries added together!

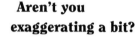

Casually worn, casually made

Off-stage, the *'layered look'* was fashionable. It might combine rolled-up, bib-fronted denim dungarees with jazzy-patterned leg-warmers, a sweater knitted in Peru, a lumberjack's check shirt and a tweed cap! From the manufacturer's point of view this fashion for floppy, untailored clothes had one *very great* advantage – you didn't need very skilled workers to make them!

Can you tell the difference?

Moustaches apart, by the early 1970s it was becoming more and more difficult to tell trend-setting MEN from WOMEN! Both wore T-shirts with slogans on them, flared trousers, 'crushed' velvet or satin jackets, 'platform sole' boots or shoes, large-collared shirts with lace cuffs, wide belts with big buckles, a gypsy's fortune in rings, chains, bracelets and ear-rings and LOTS of hair – the curlier the better. Add a wide-brimmed floppy hat and a fleecy-lined, embroidered 'Afghan' coat, and from the back you really *couldn't* tell the difference!

Loosen up!

By the mid-70s, hip-hugging trousers and waist-wrenching jackets were giving way to loose, baggy clothes. This was partly due to the influence of rock stars' stage costumes. Tight clothes showed up sweat, but loose ones allowed for padding which could soak it up!

Fit to be seen

America got the health craze and Europe soon followed. Jogging was the thing to do. But you couldn't just sweat in any old kit. An expensive 'jogging suit' was *ESSENTIAL*. Soon people who couldn't jog from the armchair to the TV found that jogging suits wore *them*. Sweatshirts were sold in huge numbers to people who *never* sweated. 'Sportswear' became 'leisurewear'. Surfing, sailing, skiing and cycling garments, made of hi-tech materials which stretched and 'breathed', were worn by people who could only *just* stretch or breathe themselves!

Do-it-yourself

The 70s saw a great boom in DIY. More people owned their own homes. Skilled craftspeople were expensive to employ. So why not '*do-it-yourself*'? In Britain some young people applied the same idea to their clothing. The result was PUNK. But, instead of making your *home* look beautiful and welcoming, you made *yourself* look ugly and frightening! Clothes were torn, slashed or picked to pieces and then covered with straps, studs and zips (which did not, of course, zip anything). After that there came the make-up – red (for eyes), black (mouth) and yellow or green (hair) – plus *SAFETY-PINS*, *CHAINS* and *RAZOR-BLADES* for the nose, ears and lips!

2000

WHATEVER NEXT?

Most past attempts to predict future fashion trends have ended up looking pretty foolish. The most successful designers have been those who stayed **just a little bit** in advance of their times. But if we can't make predictions, we can make a few good guesses!

Keep it clean

Back in the 1870s, London's best hotel had *FOUR* bathrooms between 500 guests! Nowadays we like to look and feel clean. We don't have servants to clean clothes for us, but we do have *'easy-care'* fabrics. There are already cloths which have the 'non-stick' effect used on frying pans. So we may see clothes that stains and dirt just *SLIDE* off. BAD NEWS for dry-cleaners and manufacturers of detergents!

Keep it coming round

Recycling is fashionable and good sense. One ecology group favours making jewellery out of old *CAR TYRES!* 'Grunge' has already pointed the way to recycling. This 'style' began in Seattle in 1988 and was a form of 'anti-fashion' combining garments which were too big or too small, in *VIOLENTLY* clashing patterns and colours, usually worn in layers on top of one another. By the time it reached New York in 1992 'grunge' had become high fashion, with catwalk models wearing hats made from *OLD SOCKS!* Belgian designer Martin Margiela took this idea further, ripping up second-hand clothes and stitching different parts together to make 'new' garments.

Keep it comfortable

It seems highly unlikely ANYONE will *ever* want to go back to the sort of uncomfortable clothes that were worn a century ago, such as tight corsets for women and stiff, starched collars for men! The popularity of jeans and sweatshirts shows that people want to feel RELAXED in their clothes. Specialised fibres developed for Arctic explorers, skiers and astronauts will probably become much cheaper and be used for ordinary clothes – so we won't have to wear so many layers in winter just to keep warm!

Keep it colourful

There are already materials which *CHANGE COLOUR* with changes in temperature. This might be useful in hospitals, so that nurses could see at a glance if patients had suddenly got hotter or colder. Weavers in the Middle East have known for centuries how to make textiles and carpets which *appear* to change their colour according to how they catch the light. The next step might be to have materials which change colour according to the *other* colours they are worn with!

Keep on copying

During the 1980s there were revivals of interest in the 1920s (knitwear), the 1940s (padded shoulders), the 1950s (hair-styles), the 1960s (mini-skirts) and the 1970s (flared trousers). With all the new materials there are available, how about extending the range of revivals? Comfortable *CRINOLINES?* Easy-wear *ARMOUR?*

59

Afghan coat
Long outer garment, usually made of sheep- or goat-skin; the tanned leather side is worn outwards, with the fleece as a lining.

Bale
Large roll of cloth.

Bandana
Large, brightly coloured cotton cloth, usually with a polka-dot pattern; used as a handkerchief or worn around the neck.

Bobby-socks
Short, usually white, socks; originally worn by American teenagers in the 1950s.

Breeches
Short, close-fitting trousers, usually ending at or just below the knee.

Brocade
Thick fabric, often of silk, woven with a raised pattern.

Brogue shoes
Thick leather walking shoes decorated with a punch-hole pattern.

Buckskin
Soft leather made from the skin of a deer.

Cashmere
Expensive cloth woven from the hair of a mountain-goat; originally from Kashmir in the Himalayas.

Chain mail
Armour made from interlinked rings of steel.

Chemise
Lightweight, loose-fitting dress worn as a woman's undergarment.

Choker collar
High, tight-fitting collar.

Culottes
Outer garment resembling long baggy shorts.

Deerstalker
Tweed hat with peaks at the front and back and ear-flaps that are tied over the head when not in use; originally designed for hunting.

Doublet
A tight-fitting jacket.

Drain-pipe trousers
Very tight-fitting trousers, worn by British 'Teddy Boys' in the 1950s.

Drawers
Long, baggy underpants.

Epaulet
Tab on the shoulders of a jacket or cloak; originally used to show military rank.

Girdle
Belt, usually narrow, used to tighten or hold in a garment or to hang a purse from.

Henna
Red dye; used to dye hair and to paint patterns on faces, feet and hands.

Jerkin
Sleeveless, close-fitting jacket, usually made of thick cloth or leather.

Kimono
Japanese national dress; a one-size outer garment in the shape of a wrap-over coat with wide sleeves. 'Kimono' is Japanese for 'garment'.

Moccasins
Shoes made from a single piece of soft leather; originally worn by Native Americans.

Neck-ruff
Elaborate collar of lace or muslin, usually stiffened with starch.

Plaids
Lengths of tartan cloth worn over the shoulder.

Plus-fours
Trousers, buckled at the knee, with 10 cm of cloth hanging over the buckle; usually worn for golf or hiking.

Rhinestone
An imitation diamond.

Rivets
Metal studs used to fix two layers of material tightly together.

Sari
Female outer garment, worn in India, made by draping a long, broad piece of cloth many times around the waist and then over the shoulder.

Sneakers
Lightweight rubber-soled shoes.

Trews
Scottish word for trousers, usually made of tartan-patterned cloth.

Turban
Kind of headdress made by winding a long cloth around the head several times and tucking the end in on itself.

Valet
Manservant whose duties usually include care of his employer's clothes.

INDEX